The Ninth Period

A Guidebook for Secondary School Teachers

By

Marc Hoberman

ISBN: 1-4140-2199-2 (e-book)
ISBN: 1-4140-2198-4 (Paperback)

This book is printed on acid free paper.

1stBooks - rev. 12/05/03

Dedication

I dedicate this guidebook to thousands of children who have enriched my life and to my own two children, Craig and Scott. To my wife, Ivy, I love you.

Foreword

I have been teaching for over eighteen years. I am amazed at how much I have learned from the children I teach. So many of them enable me to feel younger and even smarter. They have taught me the meaning of respect, loyalty and courage. I always said that if I won the lottery, I would become a teacher. I thought I would be a lawyer or a doctor. However, it has taken me eighteen years to realize that I did win the lottery after all.

That is why I decided to write this guidebook for new and experienced teachers alike. There should be no need to reinvent the wheel. It is my belief that the information enclosed can help you "hit the lottery" in a shorter amount of time. Most schools consist of an eight period day. I submit to you that most of teaching takes place during that extra period of time I like to call, the ninth period. Most secondary teachers work in a school where there are eight classroom periods. It is my belief that a teacher's success begins and ends with the "ninth period". This is the time before or after school when a teacher plans, meets with students, and prepares for the day.

Most people want the quick fix, so I have made this manual compact, yet informative enough to assist you in organizing your life as a teacher. I wish you luck on the path to the greatest career in America. Trust me when I say, ours is the OLDEST PROFESSION!

Best wishes,

Marc Hoberman

Many people have helped me edit and improve this guidebook. I am eternally grateful to Anthony Stephens, Lori Stiller, Lindsay Stiller, Debbie Rivera, Lenore and Syd Farber.

Table of Contents

Chapter 1-Planning

"Our whole economy is based on planned obsolescence...we make good products, we induce people to buy them, and then the next year we deliberately introduce something that will make these products old-fashioned, out of date, obsolete." Brooks Stevens

Chapter 1-Planning

"Our whole economy is based on planned obsolescence...we make good products, we induce people to buy them, and then the next year we deliberately introduce something that will make these products old-fashioned, out of date, obsolete." Brooks Stevens

As far as I can see, much of education has become "flavor of the month" oriented. This disturbs most of my colleagues because we find ourselves teaching a different type of curriculum every few years. Besides, I don't deal well with change unless I am the one initiating the change...but I digress. Luckily, the one thing that does not have to change is our persona in the classroom and the ways in which we impart information to our students. This chapter is dedicated to the planning of lessons in a way that can adapt to any content area. I have had the pleasure of teaching with "the best in the business" and have included some practices of Master Teachers in this book. Your professionalism need not ever be *obsolete*. As long as you grow constantly as an educator, you will be initiating your own changes and that is part of the formula for success in teaching.

Walk the Walk and Talk the Talk

Just like any profession, there are certain tools that you will need to look and feel like a pro. As Billy Crystal said on "Fernando's Hideaway" on *Saturday Night Live*, "It is better to look good than to feel good." When students see you in the classroom you want them, like Mr. Crystal, to say, "You look Mahvelous!." This applies to your teaching "wardrobe" as well as your clothing.

Attendance

This tool is very important. Students can't learn when they are not present. You are responsible for recording student absences and this serves many important purposes.

1. You need proof on paper of how many times a student is late or absent especially at interim report and report card time.

2. Make no mistake! Teacher attendance reports have been subpoenaed in court. Students who use your class as an alibi can see their alibi vanish if you have proof that they were not there that day. This does not happen often, but if it does, you must be prepared.

3. When you can show a student in "black and white" how much he or she is out of class or late, you have a greater chance of impacting that child.

4. In most school districts, you can't fail a student for lack of attendance. However, you can fail students for work missed during their absences.

5. For late students, try quizzes that start at the very beginning of the period and last only 5 minutes or so. Do not allow students who are late without a pass to take or make up that quiz. Their lateness is disrespectful to you, disturbing to the class, and detrimental to their grades. **The very next instance when they come in on time, thank them and congratulate them. Let them know it is a sign of maturity that they made it on time. Positive reinforcement is the key.**

Some teachers disagree with me about thanking the students and congratulating them. But, don't you feel good when someone compliments you?

Record Keeping

This section discusses a necessary evil. I used to be a very bad record keeper. I still am! Don't let that bother you. I can teach it better than I can do it. As my father used to say when I told him I would start smoking if he didn't stop, "Do as I say, not as I do." (He had emphysema for many years...I never smoked.)

Whether you are religious or not, your record book is your bible. It contains the students' names, grades, assignments, and more. You need to be organized and consistent in your approaches to record keeping. Below are some suggestions that should help you create an organized and effective record book. Make copies of your pages often in case the book is lost or stolen. Some people think they can do all this on the computer but I still like to do some things the "old-fashioned way." Remember, computers often break down and lose power and files.

1. Set up each page in alphabetical order. One page per class.

2. I like to skip a space or two between each letter. For example, If I have four students whose last names begin with the letter "S", I skip one line or more before I start the letter "T". The reason behind this is simple. Children leave and enter my class throughout the year because they move, and I hate to cross out names every quarter or add new students to the bottom of the list. Another good idea is to write the names in pencil.

3. I like to number my homework assignments and therefore list them in my record book by number and actual assignment and date. This way, if a student wishes to make up an assignment, (don't laugh, sometimes they want to make up missed work) I can look up the date, or the assignment number rather quickly.

4. I know teachers who have a separate notebook for each class with one page set aside for each student. They keep these anecdotals and record student

performance, behavior, phone calls and have a PAPER TRAIL for each student. I did this one year when I worked in a middle school and it worked phenomenally well. It is a lot of work, however, but well worth the effort. Students are shocked during a parental visit when you point out something they did two months ago. Hint: Try to record positive behaviors and experiences as well. **Positive reinforcement is the key.**

Lessons

It is now "meat and potatoes" time. I believe you must have a good lesson plan that is organized and well thought out in order to present a good lesson to your students. However, I do **not** agree that this plan must conform to your school, district or chairperson's format. Unfortunately, especially for untenured teachers, you may be forced to adhere to a set format or template when creating your lesson plan.

My philosophy is that a lesson plan is only as good as the teacher. A great lesson plan on paper means absolutely nothing if the person instructing is lethargic, not respected by the students, and ineffective. Below are the elements of a lesson plan format that I use in the classroom.

Aim:

The aim is always posed in the form of a question. This should not be a question that can be answered with a yes or no response. It is my hope that students will NOT know the answer at the beginning of the lesson, but will be able to answer the aim out loud or in their minds by the time the lesson is completed.

Do Now:

This should be a review of the previous day's work or something that the students can do for five minutes or so that directly relates to the present day's assignment. This is a great time for you to take attendance, collect homework, and answer any student questions. (Sound like a lot? Welcome to teaching.)

Motivation:

I usually think of a question related to the lesson that will stir some sort of discussion in the room. You must have backup questions in case no one answers your initial question. This rarely happens. (I am being sarcastic. It always happens, so be prepared.)

Development:

This is the part where you actually teach the lesson. Hopefully there will be note taking and discussion. Of course, there will be questions but you must be sure to get through the lesson. I am sure you will have a set curriculum to get through by the end of the year so keep the kids and yourself on task.

Summary:

This usually takes two minutes as you try to have students summarize what they have learned. I do not advocate lecturing to kids and therefore like to hear THEM do the summary. I know that I understood the material but did they? Make sure and let them prove it to you. They are your critics and if they learned, then you earned yourself a four star review!

Following is an example of a lesson I have done while teaching Shakespeare's *Romeo and Juliet*.

Aim: Why is Romeo considered to be Petrarchan in his actions?

(The students do not know who Petrarch is at this point)

Do Now: Write a brief journal entry describing what true "love" means to you.

Motivation: What is the difference between love and infatuation?

(There is usually discussion here and we finally come to a definition TOGETHER that infatuation is when you are so taken by someone that you do not see his or her faults, while love is accepting people for their faults and loving and accepting them anyway.)

Development:

a. Petrarch-Italian poet who wrote about love. Petrarch was in love with love just as Romeo loves to be in love. Romeo has just ended a relationship with a young girl as he meets and immediately falls in love with Juliet.

b. Petrarchan sonnets dealt with love and because we see that Romeo is always passionate about someone he is seen as a Petrarchan lover.

c. We then read the next part of the play that shows how passionate Romeo is and how he is the essence of love and passion in a human being.

d. After the reading I summarize by referring back to the Aim.

e. I then assign the homework and ask for questions. Always ask if the students understand the homework assignment. This way they can't tell you the next day that they couldn't do the homework because they didn't understand it. (Now that you eliminated that excuse, you have to work on the others.)

I had a student who couldn't do his homework because his grandmother died. After speaking with my colleagues I found out that he was a most unlucky child because his grandmother died eight times in the month of April. How unfortunate!

Speaking of homework, don't give homework just for the sake of homework. Make it meaningful or the students will see it as a waste of time. I usually read the responses out loud, (without disclosing names), so they know I read it and they learn from their classmates. I usually don't give homework on Fridays. I tell the students I want to give them some time to relax over the weekend since I give homework Monday-Thursday. To be truthful, I don't like to come back to a lot of papers on Monday morning. I deserve a break too! (See Chapter 10.)

Tests and Quizzes

Tests and quizzes should be challenging and check for understanding of the material that was taught. This is not your opportunity to trick the students but rather to make sure that they know the material and can apply it appropriately. I once had an entire class fail my test and I was proud that I was able to fool them. I soon realized that I did not fool them at all. They fooled me into thinking that I taught the information correctly. I tossed the papers in the garbage and told the students we both needed to do our jobs better. On the next test, I had a seventy- percent passing rate. This was a low-level class and no small feat.

Following the Curriculum

More often than not, there is a standardized test lurking in the distance waiting to pounce on our students at a moment's notice. We are responsible for teaching our students information and strategies that will enable them to reach their full potentials on a variety of exams in many disciplines. This is a necessary evil and we need to realize that we do not teach in a vacuum.

You need to familiarize yourself with the curriculum. Feel free to ask as many questions as necessary. Ask your colleagues and your chairperson or Assistant Principal. Leave no stone unturned. After all, every finger will be pointed at you if your kids do not achieve. Keep a log of whom you asked and what the responses were so you have proof that you asked for help.

Audio and Video in the Classroom

I love the use of audio and visual aids in the classroom. Technology has come so far that it is silly not to take advantage of how you can utilize it in your lessons.

You have audio, visual, kinesthetic, tactile, and other learners in your classrooms and you need to address the many learning styles of these children as efficiently as possible.

Audio: I use tapes and now mostly CD's of song lyrics, speeches, and lines in plays to help get my point across. With the Internet and CD burners, there is virtually no limit to what you can bring into the classroom setting.

Video: I love to use video in the classroom but I am very much against the ever so popular "plug 'n play" method employed by far too many teachers. I always supply students with a study guide that they have to follow and answer while the video is on. I often stop the VCR at key points and have a brief discussion about the material covered.

Interactive Teaching

Graphic Organizers
VCR
CD or Tape Player
Overhead Projector
Socratic Seminar
Proxima (hooked up to the computer)
Smart Board (This is wild. It's a board that is a giant computer.)

The above items add so much to the teaching experience and help to motivate students. Most students do not need to be motivated. They are alive and energetic and always ready for action.........NOT!

Note Taking

I feel that I am always growing as an educator and am learning constantly. Note taking is definitely an area in which I stray from the average teacher. First of all, my handwriting is terrible. Secondly, I believe that if you teach something properly, students will remember it...plain and simple. Students do not take notes during their favorite song or movie but are still able to regurgitate everything down to the finest detail. Why is that? Because it was interesting! I don't believe that the average student even knows how to take notes effectively and that is why I address it in my *Speed Reading and Study Skills Seminar*. They certainly don't study from their notes correctly so if you are big on notes, you need to monitor their work.

1. I used to check notebooks as part of the quarter grade. BORING!!!

2. A teacher once showed me how she gave Notebook quizzes. I ask four questions on a sheet of paper. The students have four minutes to answer all of the questions. If their notebook is organized, they will have no trouble receiving

a 100. If they are disorganized, they are up NOTEBOOK CREEK without a paddle. After all, just two incorrect answers will result in a failing grade of 50.

3. An example of questions follow:

   a. What was the Aim on October 10th?
   b. What was the name of the author we studied on October 12th?
   c. What was Homework Assignment #14?
   d. What is the definition of personification as written on October 18th?

If children were absent, they are still responsible for the work so I do not excuse them from the quiz. This MOTIVATES them to get the work they missed since this is the easiest 100 they will ever see. This works for Notebook Quizzes in all subjects.

I tell students to get the name and phone number of at least two students in the class so they can call them for work when they are absent. This was a given "back in the day" when I went to school but children feel they should be exempt from any work if they were absent. Let them know that you missed them, and that they missed an assignment. Accountability is very important in education!

Socratic Seminars

I am absolutely in love with this method of teaching. It works for any discipline and any age level. It brings out the maturity in the students and it feels like you are in a college setting. To help the students, use the A-Z sheet at the back of the guidebook for them to list characters and adjectives, nouns, etc. This is how I first introduce it to the students.

"Today we are going to learn about Socratic Seminars. Socrates was a philosopher who not only taught his students, but learned from them as well. We are going to get in a circle and answer questions based on the material we are currently working on. You can pass if you wish but you cannot pass twice. Once you answer the question, others will help you expand your answer."

All students are then instructed to take out a piece of paper and write their names on it and fold it over so it stands up in front of their desks. I am the FACILITATOR of the seminar NOT the teacher. I have questions prepared and ask them to prepare one question on their own. We then go in order, clockwise.

The answers are amazing. The circle brings us together as a team and we have incredible discussions. A variation I created is to put one student in the middle and the other students ask him or her questions. You get one point for a correct response and one point for stumping a student. If you stump someone, you go in the middle. The person with the most points at the end of the period wins a prize. (A coupon for a slice of pizza, extra points, and so on.)

Assemblies

Some people don't feel that this is part of your lesson but I disagree. I tell the students that they will walk in two lines in the hall, boys on one side and girls on the other side. These are high school kids and they don't like this but it really works.

Because of my humorous rapport with my students, I threaten to make those who talk hold hands on the way to the assembly. They always laugh at this, so be sure they know you are kidding.

Always sit with your kids at the assembly. There are too many teachers who stand by the wall as if they don't want to be near their kids. The smartest people I have ever met in education are the students themselves. If you don't like them, they will know it before you do. You may want to sit next to the ones who usually have the most difficulty keeping quiet. They feel your presence and will be better behaved at the assembly.

NOTES

NOTES

Chapter 2-Classroom Management

"It has always been my contention that no one has a corner on brains. The greatest feats in business, as in virtually all of life, are performed by very ordinary, normal men and women. Not geniuses. Peak experiences of ordinary, normal people create leaders in business and elsewhere." Harold Geneen, <u>Managing</u>.

Chapter 2-Classroom Management

"It has always been my contention that no one has a corner on brains. The greatest feats in business, as in virtually all of life, are performed by very ordinary, normal men and women. Not geniuses. Peak experiences of ordinary, normal people create leaders in business and elsewhere." Harold Geneen, Managing.

Teaching is rewarding, exciting, and often fun. But make no mistake; teaching is a business. We compete for salaries with other districts and cities, federal funding is often based on attendance, and some districts have been known to deny people tenure in order to hire a new, less experienced teacher. This hurts the kids, but keeps some taxpayers happy. Harold Geneen is correct in saying that we all have the power to create leaders. However, if you don't have ownership and control of your classroom, you will never get the chance to impart knowledge.

I have seen teachers who were absolutely brilliant in their content. Unfortunately, they did not have the management skills to create a learning environment in their classrooms. This chapter should help all teachers, novice and seasoned, create a learning environment rich in knowledge and respect.

Managing Student Behavior

I remember when I first began to teach. I was lucky enough to be part of a subschool where the toughest dean resided. She was respected and feared by the students. She laughed when years later I told her she scared me as well. When the kids misbehaved, a daily occurrence, I said I would send for her and they quieted down rather quickly. One day I threatened to call her and they continued their poor behavior and even began throwing spitballs at me. I soon found out what they already knew. She was absent! I never had control of my class; she did.

I immediately asked teachers with excellent class control if I could observe their techniques during my lunch hour. I sat and learned from the Masters and over the years I have honed my own skills to create what I think is a very powerful formula for managing student behavior.

It is not difficult to teach in a classroom where students are misbehaving. It is IMPOSSIBLE! The following is a step-by-step approach to managing student behavior.

First, all students get a contract the first day of class. You have to decide on your rules; I can't do that for you. I often ask what rule number three is as part of my Notebook Quiz. You can ask any number on a Notebook Quiz (Always number your rules so you can direct them to the rule they broke quickly.) Some of my rules include:

1. No foul language
2. No hats (Bad hair days are your problem, not mine.)
3. Raise your hand to ask or answer a question
4. Never throw your work out
5. Garbage gets thrown out at the end of the period (I hate when they get up and throw garbage away when I am teaching. It distracts me and is rude.)
6. You are responsible for all work even if you are absent
7. The period is over when I say so, the bell means nothing to me. (I do not allow kids to pack up before I dismiss class. Those who do are made to leave last.)
8. Bring a Loose-leaf Notebook, two pens and two pencils EVERY day.
(I don't lend pens, I rent supplies. They cost points or a phone call home. I used to take money but not anymore.)

I have them sign the contract and the parent signs as well. I then make copies of the contract and keep one set and return the others to the students. They have to keep it in their notebooks. I like to have an outline in front of me indicating the rules I would like to be in my contract. However, I allow the students to create some of the rules that will be part of the contract for several reasons:

1. Their rules are usually more stringent than mine.
2. They take class very seriously when they have taken part in the creation of the contract.
3. This allows them to have OWNERSHIP of some of the management of the classroom.

If someone breaks a rule I never answer in a negative way. I am sarcastic and they find this humorous and always apologize. For example, if someone calls out an answer I say, "What part of **don't** call out are you having trouble with. Is it the word **"don't?"** Or I might say, "Feel free to call out." They know I am being facetious and quickly apologize.

If someone gets up to throw out the garbage I say to that person, "Do me a favor, remind me when we throw garbage away." They know this is a rhetorical question and hold the paper until class is over. This way, I make it the student's decision to follow the rules, not mine.

Let students know that their signature means that they are agreeing to follow the rules as set forth by you. You are counting on them to be true to their word and honor their commitment. In fact, when they arrive late to class, I have them sign a late sheet that I keep on a clipboard. They will be signing many contracts in their lives and this is the first of many. Although I want to set an example in my class, I sometimes throw garbage out during the period and they ask me to repeat the rule since I just broke it. When this happens, they are truly taking ownership of the rules.

Allow me to get this off my chest. While I agree that we need to be role models for our children, I don't believe I need to leave **my** beeper at home. We are no longer children and we must teach them that with certain jobs and situations, certain privileges exist. We have gone to school, graduated and followed all of the rules. Now it is their turn. I tell them they will be learning how changes are made and they will do this when they become teachers or leaders in other chosen professions. I also mention that well educated people have been changing rules for centuries, so they are in good company.

I have learned my greatest lessons and techniques from other teachers. In turn, I like to think that many teachers have learned from me as well. Below is a wonderful system for rewarding students that I learned from a master teacher twelve years ago and people have learned it from me. It's ok to pass the baton and share ideas.

The Check System

I am going to introduce this system in dialogue format. This is almost exactly how I introduce it to my students.

On top of the date on your papers you will write a check every time I tell you to take one. You get checks for correct answers, innovative questions, lending a pen or pencil to a classmate, giving a classmate the make-up assignments and for anything else positive and mature that you do. Checks are your key to success in my class. They boost your average. If you have a 63 average, you will fail my class, However, if you have a fair amount of checks, I will give you at least two more points so you can pass. A 77 is not a great average but a lot of checks will enable you to get an 80.

I will call for checks every two weeks. It is your responsibility to record checks properly. Some of you may wonder how I keep you from cheating and writing down more checks than you have. It's simple. I secretly memorize the checks of the same three people for two weeks. If your checks don't match mine, then the following occurs.

1. You lose your checks for one month
2. Your parent must come in
3. You and I meet with the dean, or chairperson or Assistant Principal

I take checks seriously and so should you. They earn you much needed points and they cost me money. Every quarter the person with the most checks gets a CD of his or her choice. (No Adult Content CD's allowed.)

(Teachers can vary the rewards as their money will allow. I often give rewards and certificates for most improved checks as well.)

When someone does something that deserves a check I simply say, "Take a check." Sometimes I will offer many checks for one answer if the question is a more difficult one.

After a few months, students are told to take checks automatically as they know they truly deserve them. When they are able to monitor themselves, a real partnership has developed.

Please don't tell anybody this but I never really keep track of checks. If a poor student calls in 80 checks and I know he or she rarely ever gets any, then I challenge that student. All students, elementary through high school love the check system. It is positive reinforcement at its best and they compete to get them. Be consistent and diligent in giving out and collecting checks. Be proactive and tell a student that he or she had a "C" average and now earned a "B" because of the checks. Remember, checks are only good for two weeks. Students have to start a brand new count every two weeks.

A variation of this method is to award coupons or fake money. Then the students can buy things such as a free homework, points on a test and so on. I never use checks against a child. For example, I never say, "Take away 10 checks because you were bad today." Once students earn a check, it is theirs to keep.

This also fosters more class participation. I was a shy student as a child so I am always cognizant of shy students I teach. Therefore, I give checks for a good homework, good behavior and other things in case shy students don't like to raise their hands to answer or ask a question.

Remember: **Positive Reinforcement is the key**.

Seating Charts

I let students sit where they want the first day I meet them and then I ask if anyone needs to sit in the front due to vision problems. I always fill up the seats in front of me because I like to have a bunch of students near me when I teach and I don't like them all over the room. I have used a Delaney books, and I highly recommend them. You can switch seats with a single card maneuver and you can keep attendance on the back of the cards, There is also a space for student data such as name, phone number, and address.

Charts are also very helpful to substitutes. This is a good time to mention that you should leave a copy of your seating chart in a folder with a copy of your contract for your substitute. Leave an easy to follow lesson plan as well. Create these ahead of time in case of last minute absences on your part.

Cultural Respect

Students should not treat each other with disrespect in your presence, ever. If you hear a comment and ignore it, I believe that is the same as you saying the comment yourself. Get angry and get serious...fast. I don't believe in the, "how would you like it if he called you that?" approach. Frankly, I don't care how the other kid likes it. I don't like it and I do not tolerate it. I don't tell people that I don't see color in my classroom because I do. Everyone is not the same. We are all unique individuals. I work in a culturally diverse school and I have learned a tremendous amount about different religions and cultures and this is the most important lesson we can teach.

Writing Up Negative Behavior

When students misbehave in my classroom I always try to handle the problem myself. I call the student out of the room. I often get asked, "Why can't you talk to me here?" My answer is, "What I want to discuss with you is nobody else's business and I am willing to give you my undivided attention so I would appreciate yours for a minute." **Never** get into an argument with a student in front of the class. You will always lose. If you have to prove that you are in charge, then you are not in charge. People who are in control of their room don't need to prove it, everybody knows.

When I write up a student's behavior I usually read it to the student and leave it on my desk. I tell him or her that if he can change his behavior for the rest of the period, I will tear up the form. However, there will be no other chance. Actions speak louder than words so if they say, "OK" I answer, I know you can behave, just show me that I am right. Ninety percent of the time I am able to tear up the written form. When a dean gets a complaint from me, it is taken very seriously. I don't send gum chewers and other small infractions to someone else. Handle your own problems and soon you will see that you don't have any.

For example, I do not allow students to put their heads down in my classroom. I never allow them to sleep. Some teachers do, believe it or not, but this is highly unprofessional. I take the student outside of the room and say, "If something at home is creating an atmosphere where you can't get enough rest at night, perhaps I can help you. But, you cannot sleep in my room. I am responsible for your education and sleeping is not part of that education, sorry. Let me know if I can help you with any problems that are making you so tired."

I put the onus on them to learn. I also let them know that I take their education seriously and will make them take it seriously as well. My statement that I am willing to help them diffuses any anger they may have. My saying, "sorry" gives the appearance that I wish they could rest in my room, but it is not a possibility since I take my job, and their education, most seriously. Then I thank them.

Of course, serious infractions need to be handled seriously.

Go to the rooms where learning is always taking place. Learn from the Masters. Pick their brains. It's an incredible compliment to them and most are eager to help you. Borrow, Learn, and Pass It On!

NOTES

NOTES

Chapter 3-Observations

Alexander Pope (1688—1744)

"To observations which ourselves we make,
We grow more partial for th' observer's sake."

Chapter 3-Observations

Alexander Pope (1688—1744)

"To observations which ourselves we make, We grow more partial for th' observer's sake."

Pre-Conference

An informal observation may consist of a pre-conference with your chairperson. You will discuss your lesson and the elements that you feel will make it effective. Typically non-tenured teachers have six observations a year. Two each semester by the chairperson and one each semester by the principal. Tenured teacher observations vary from school to school. It's usually one a year but some schools allow colleagues to write the evaluations.

Often, the chairperson and/or principal walk in unannounced. It would be silly for me to tell you not to worry. I would be right, but you wouldn't listen. I still get butterflies in my stomach and really want to be able to "strut my stuff".

1. Make eye contact with the students. Don't be too "touchy feely" with the kids but I sometimes give a pat on the back or shoulder for good work.

2. Use the Arrow of Recitation. This is when you take one response and "shoot" it to another student. This way, the students are helping each other build answers.

3. Calling all students, calling all students…Include as many students as possible. Observations usually include the number of student responses and how many different students responded.

4. Feel free to use humor. Don't use humor if you don't usually use it.

5. Don't be a **different** teacher during an observation. Show the real you, not the Vegas version.

6. Dress appropriately but this is my philosophy on a daily basis, not just on observation days.

7. If you know about the observation ahead of time, tell your students they MAY have a visitor who needs to check on their performance. Say nothing more.

8. Don't be embarrassed by inappropriate comments made by the students. Don't ignore them either. You can simply say, "That wasn't appropriate Steven." Then move on.

9. Make sure to give a typed version of your lesson plan to the person observing you.

10. At the Post Observation Conference, listen to all suggestions made. Do not be alarmed by negative feedback for two reasons:

    a. Your chairperson HAS to make suggestions.
    b. Some administrators just don't know how to give feedback properly.

11. Always incorporate some of their suggestions in your next lesson that they will be observing. Feel free to let them know that your suggestion helped you make the lesson even better. You really can learn how to get better through the eyes of another.

12. Be prepared to tell the observer your thoughts on the lesson. You will often be asked how you think the lesson went and how you could have improved it even before you hear any comments from the person doing your observation.

I once knew a Master Teacher who was observed and gave an excellent lesson. She was told that next time her window shades had to be at least three inches above the windowsill. Some people grasp at straws and just don't know how to say, "good job". Many administrators are known to be very helpful during this process so just be patient and calm and you will be fine.

I remember a time when a teacher had an appointment to be observed and the Assistant Principal had a last minute emergency and did not show up. Later in the hall, the TENURED teacher said, "I hope next time you tell me in advance when you are going to cancel. I wasted a perfectly good lesson on those kids!"

NOTES

NOTES

Chapter 4-Dealing With Parents

"Parents love their children more than children love their parents."
Medieval Proposition

Chapter 4-Dealing With Parents

"Parents love their children more than children love their parents." Medieval Proposition

Just because kids say their parents don't care does not make it true. I have yet to see a parent who does not care. I have seen frustrated parents, parents that were too young, and overworked parents. But uncaring parents…not yet.

I have not been at all satisfied with the amount of parents that come to open school night. However, I recently learned that some cultures believe that the schools are the all knowing and that parents trust us implicitly to care for and educate their children while they are in school. Does your school welcome parents? Do you attend PTA meetings? Try to get involved in Parent Involvement in your school. They can be your greatest allies.

Be truthful when speaking with parents but be professional. Log all phone calls listing the date and time you called and list the name of the person with whom you spoke.

There are several ways to tell a parent bad news.

1. If a student is misbehaving, I always call the parent in his or her presence. I make the student dial the phone and ask for the parent. This way the parent doesn't think that the child is injured and the school is calling for really bad news.

2. Use what I call, "professional synonyms". Others call these euphemisms. Instead of saying, "Hi, Mrs. Jones, your son is a lying cheater. He copied off someone else's paper during a test. I can never trust him again."

You could say, "Hello Mrs. Jones, I am sorry to have to bother you with this, but your son has left me no alternative. He copied answers from another student's test paper today. I feel that if he spent more time studying, he wouldn't have to rely on the answers of others. I would like to suggest that you talk to him about being better prepared for tests. If there is any way you think I could be of help please call me or drop me a note."

I then tell the student that I am deeply disappointed that he cheated. I do not respect that and I really expect more from him. If he does study and performs well on the next test, be sure to let the parent know. If you really want to throw parents for a loop, call them with good news. I am fairly certain that less than 5% of parent phone calls are positive. It might be time consuming, but it is invaluable.

Letters Home

Be very careful with what you put in writing. A good method is to have your chairperson countersign any notes home. This way they will be able to troubleshoot any problematic phrases. Also, if you get called in for a letter deemed inappropriate, you can prove that you went through the proper channels.

I like to use a checklist and a form letter. (Use school letterhead)

To the parent of_____

Please note that your son/daughter is having trouble in the following areas.

_____ homework
_____ classwork
_____ behavior
_____ etc…

Have your chairperson or AP sign the original and then you can make copies. You might want to make copies of letters you send home to keep for your records.

When you meet with parents, you may notice that they sometimes seem confrontational. They are often intimidated. They don't know how their child is performing and they may have had negative experiences in the past.

1. Smile when you first meet them. A sincere smile puts people at ease. (A fake smile makes people nauseous.)

2. Be as positive as you can and begin with the positive. Thank them for coming. These people sometimes have to lose wages to visit the school. I know it is their child and their responsibility, but if they care, you have a great start. Then, if there is something negative to say, be gentle, yet firm.

3. Don't just cry about all the bad things the student is doing. Don't mention a negative aspect about the student's performance unless you can offer a solution as to how you can all work together to help him or her improve. If possible, try to ask in advance if the student can join you.

4. I always say with the student present, "Have I said anything that isn't true?" I rarely have a student who disagrees because I have set the tone for improvement. I do not allow for a gripe session. We are there to explore solutions. Remember: **Positive reinforcement is the key**.

NOTES

NOTES

Chapter 5- Administration

"Every country has the government it deserves." Josephe de Maistre

Chapter 5- Administration

"Every country has the government it deserves." Josephe de Maistre

Bosses and supervisors are part of any business, and teaching is no exception. Administrators can be helpful and patient. Others can be a hindrance and impatient as well. Nevertheless, you need to manage their expectations as well as your own and you will find yourself working for the administrator you deserve.

1. All administrators were once teachers. However, they tend to forget what it was like to be in your shoes. In their defense, they have to work with all teachers and some teachers are not professional and are often difficult to deal with. As much as I love having tenure, there are some educators who hide behind it and do not earn their salary. It is difficult for administrators to remove a tenured teacher who is inept and they are often frustrated by this fact.

2. I have been in an administrative position of sorts when I ran a Peer Mediation Program for the district and the pressure is enormous.

3. However, no one has the right to speak down to you and you deserve respect, even from your superiors.

4. If you are truly doing your job to the best of your ability, you will find that most administrators will back you up whenever possible. Understand though, that education is VERY political and people do what is best for them and whatever makes them look good in the eyes of THEIR superiors.

5. Try to make things easier for your superiors. If you can, try to help out when they need someone "in a pinch". Offer to help cover a class when a teacher leaves at the last minute due to an emergency. Help during assemblies. This is not simply a brown-nosing technique. (All of my closest friends think I am the world's biggest kiss up but I actually like being involved and helping out.)

If you do your best job, then you will be seen as someone who can be counted on. Be pleasant, be professional, and give and command respect from all with whom you work.

Chapter 6- Colleagues

"If the finished parts are going to work together, they must be developed by groups that share a common picture of what each part must accomplish. Engineers in different disciplines are forced to communicate; the challenge of management and team-building is to make that communication happen."
K. Eric Drexler

Chapter 6- Colleagues

"If the finished parts are going to work together, they must be developed by groups that share a common picture of what each part must accomplish. Engineers in different disciplines are forced to communicate; the challenge of management and team-building is to make that communication happen."
K. Eric Drexler

You need to work together as a faculty in order for the "finished product" (the students) to learn to work together and be successful.

The Good, The Bad, and The Ugly

If you thought some of the kids were nuts...You ain't seen nothing yet!!!

A school is usually like a small city unto itself. Many faculties are very close and rely on each other for emotional survival. Some of your peers, however, will need to be medicated. I love teaching because I love to gossip. There is a plethora of stories to be had in a school and there is no dearth of material.

The Good

There are so many good teachers who are also wonderful people who have taught me so much about education. Many people who have helped me avoid some serious situations have counseled me. To them, I am eternally grateful. This is not a career in which you can succeed alone. Take every bit of help you can get.

The Bad

Oh boy, this can get nasty. Suffice it to say that several teachers I know went into teaching for two reasons: July and August. They don't like kids and, trust me, kids do not like them. I don't know how they lasted, but this is my philosophy. Our students will grow up to be the leaders of tomorrow. They may have horrible supervisors and bosses along the way and they will become successful in spite of these losers. Thank god for the bad teachers, they make it easier to pick out the good ones.

The Ugly

I have seen teachers degrade children.
I have seen teachers curse at students.
I have seen teachers hit students.

There are bad people in every profession. We can only hope that the powers that be will weed out the undesirables as quickly as possible. I can't tell you what to do when you witness a colleague act unprofessionally. You must do what your heart tells you...no more, no less. Do what you must in order to sleep peacefully at night.

NOTES

NOTES

Chapter 7-Collaborative Teaching

"There is no "I" in TEAM."

Chapter 7-Collaborative Teaching

"There is no "I" in TEAM." Somebody said this, but I don't know who, sorry.

A book would not be able to cover this topic, but I do want to mention it since:

a. I have done it for over five years
b. I believe in it wholeheartedly and feel it will be used more in the future

In the best case scenario, if you teach collaboratively, you will be able to choose your partner, but this is not always the case. I didn't really get to choose my co-teacher but god smiled on me and I got an angel. I don't mention other teachers in this guidebook, but you can see a picture of her if you go to my website, hint, hint. gradesuccessinc.com

You need to respect each other and respect what each of you can bring to the teaching table. It is important to divide and conquer whenever possible. If you think that two people in the classroom reduces your workload, you are sadly mistaken.

You need to do lesson plans together and constantly discuss students in depth. This is a difficult job to do with someone else, but I think it is invaluable to the students. Just think of all the things that have to be delegated.

Attendance
Grades
Lesson planning
Parental contact
And more…

There are many collaborative teaching approaches.

1. One teaches, one roams
2. Both teach different parts of the lesson
3. One does the content and one focuses on various learning styles

Many times you have to learn your rhythm, "on the fly". You can't create this winning team overnight. My co-teacher and I weren't really comfortable until our third year together. We are always in the process of tweaking and refining our approaches.

The most difficult thing for me was to give up some of my territory. As I mentioned before, I tend to be territorial. Now, I am happy to let my co-teacher share the responsibility of delivering the lesson. It gives me time to visit with each student personally during the class period. I feel that I am truly bonding with the students. If done right, Collaborative Teaching can be very rewarding.

NOTES

NOTES

Chapter 8-Emergency Situations

"She felt that those who prepared for all the emergencies of life beforehand may equip themselves at the expense of joy."
Howard's End

Chapter 8-Emergency Situations

"She felt that those who prepared for all the emergencies of life beforehand may equip themselves at the expense of joy." Howard's End

You can't spend your entire teaching career planning for what might happen. However, you can be informed and prepared for certain situations.

Fights

If you don't see a fight in your teaching career, then the school you are teaching in doesn't have any students. I have witnessed fights between faculty members, parents and security, teachers and students and, of course, students against students. I broke up a fight between a student and substitute teacher once and the student missed the teacher and tossed a desk on my foot. I broke my instep and spent five weeks at home eating Twinkies and watching General Hospital. (At least I got to see Luke and Laura's wedding.)

In the past, we were encouraged to breakup fights. Now we are told that we are not covered (insured) if we get hurt while breaking up a fight since this is not part of our job description. We are supposed to secure the room and wait for security. You need to tell students that this is an emergency situation and in a firm voice usher them where you wish them to be.

The only time I jump in any more is if one of the disputants is getting brutally beaten. Please do not misunderstand. These type of fights are few and far between, but you need to know what you are going to do because the safety of others is in your hands.

Any drugs, weapons or sexual misconduct to which you are privy must be reported immediately. Be sure to document to whom you spoke and when. If someone is being abused at home and you do not report it, you and the school district can be sued! Always log everything. These "paper trails" can be very helpful to you.

In today's world, there are so many things that can go wrong, we need to focus on what can go right. However, the Boy Scout motto, "Be Prepared" can be applied to every aspect of teaching. You have chosen a career where the things that go on inside your classroom during a lesson are only a small percentage of what your job truly entails. The work is exhausting but extremely rewarding.

Our final chapters pertain to the two most important aspects of teaching:

The Students, and YOU!

NOTES

NOTES

Chapter 9-The Students
(The 2nd most important factor)

"The children [on TV] are too well behaved and are reasonable beyond their years. All the children pop in with exceptional insights. On many of the shows the children's insights are apt to be unexpectedly philosophical. The lesson seems to be, 'Listen to little children carefully and you will learn great truths.'"
G. Weinberg.

Chapter 9-The Students
(The 2nd most important factor)

"The children [on TV] are too well behaved and are reasonable beyond their years. All the children pop in with exceptional insights. On many of the shows the children's insights are apt to be unexpectedly philosophical. The lesson seems to be, 'Listen to little children carefully and you will learn great truths.'" G. Weinberg.

There are no words to describe the joy I have received from teaching children. Shaping the minds of our future is just a small part of the satisfaction. Their thoughts and beliefs keep me young and I have learned more from them than I can ever impart to others.

I began my teaching career in a school with 6th, 7th and 8th graders. They overcame so many obstacles just to walk in the door each morning. I can't imagine that kind of courage. The day before I wrote this chapter I went into New York City with my wife and children to view the horrid destruction of what was once the Twin Towers. Even my sons were quiet and solemn as we viewed the debris. We then read through the many signs and remembrances that were posted. Later, I took my children to the Pokemon Center in Rockefeller Plaza. There, not one, but two former students I had taught fifteen years earlier approached me to thank me for being a good teacher. They said they learned a lot and laughed a lot in my classroom. I introduced them to my family whom they had never met.

These girls were 28 years old and said that they were still trying to get good jobs and earn enough money to move into better neighborhoods. I truly believe that education is the cure to our nation's ills. I hope that some day we have all the money we need for education and we have to hold a bake sale in order to buy weapons for our armies.

You will come across hundreds and even thousands of students in your career. They are all unique. The quiet ones deserve your attention just as much as the seemingly more personable ones. If you just think about the wonderful teachers you still admire, I am sure you can understand what I mean. RAISE YOUR EXPECTATIONS. Demand the best that your kids have to offer. When your students know you expect 100%, they respect you because you are showing that you respect them. **NOBODY RISES TO LOW EXPECTATIONS......NOBODY!**

Take the time to get to know your students above and beyond what their grades tell you. They come from interesting families, they have incredible hobbies and stories that they can share with you. The best way to do this is to create a safe environment in your classroom. Some people mistake this "safety" as simply physical. Your students must feel **physically** AND **emotionally** safe with you.

They need to feel that they are able to learn from their mistakes. Do this, and your rewards will never end and you will be responsible for helping to create productive members of our society. Invest in our kids, it beats any mutual fund I have ever seen.

NOTES

NOTES

Chapter 10-YOU!!!
(The MOST Important factor)

No quote is needed here. **You are the most important piece in the puzzle.** Over 50% of inner city teachers quit before they have completed five years of service. An inner city teacher ranks in the top three of the most stressful careers. Teachers in the suburbs have an enormous amount of stress as well. Just consider:

1. Dealing with the students
2. Rising to the expectations of the district
3. Answering to the parents
4. Working for hours on lesson plans
5. Going to graduate school to earn more credits so you can earn more money

These are just some of the myriad of things that are part of a teaching career. You probably won't get rich from teaching. However, there is money to be made in curriculum writing, tutoring, publishing articles and more. My guess is that if you were solely motivated by money then you wouldn't be reading this guidebook in the first place.

You must take care of yourself both physically and emotionally. You should always be reading a pleasure book. As Emily Dickinson writes, "There is no frigate like a book, to take us lands away." If your life is all about your work, then forgive me for saying this, but you don't have much of a life. You deserve a life outside of the classroom. See movies, travel, and learn how to relieve stress.

An Exercise for You

Proper breathing is the best way to relieve stress. Be seated comfortably and close your eyes and inhale slowly and deeply. Now exhale slowly and fully until you can't expend any more air. Repeat this process slowly two to four times. Then breathe normally for two minutes or so. Focus on the number one and concentrate deeply.

If the number starts disappearing, focus on the number two. You will feel very relaxed when this is over. If you feel dizzy during any part of this exercise, stop! Be sure you are not breathing in and out too quickly during the first part of this relaxation technique.

Always learn. Read books about your profession. Attend workshops of YOUR choice and always know that you can be a better teacher no matter how many years you have spent in the classroom. You are a special human being because you have dedicated your life to helping children. I know you will feel as successful and fulfilled as I still do after eighteen years. I look forward to the next eighteen. Thank you for giving me the opportunity to share my thoughts and beliefs with you. Good luck in your career and remember...**Positive Reinforcement is the Key!**

NOTES

NOTES

Student Check Sheet
Class_____ Period____

Name	Dates:	Dates:	Dates:	Dates:	Dates:	Dates:

Marc Hoberman

Date: Class: Period: Teacher:

AIM:

DO NOW:

MOTIVATION:

DEVELOPMENT:

KEY TERMS:

SUMMARY:

HOMEWORK:

Following is an example of a lesson I have done while teaching Shakespeare's *Romeo and Juliet*.

Aim: Why is Romeo considered to be Petrarchan in his actions?

(The students do not know who Petrarch is at this point)

Do Now: Write a brief journal entry describing what true "love" means to you.

Motivation: What is the difference between love and infatuation?

(There is usually discussion here and we finally come to a definition TOGETHER that infatuation is when you are so taken by someone that you do not see his or her faults, while love is accepting people for their faults and loving and accepting them anyway.)

Development:

f. Petrarch-Italian poet who wrote about love. Petrarch was in love with love just as Romeo loves to be in love. Romeo has just ended a relationship with a young girl as he meets and immediately falls in love with Juliet.

g. Petrarchan sonnets dealt with love and because we see that Romeo is always passionate about someone he is seen as a Petrarchan lover.

h. We then read the next part of the play that shows how passionate Romeo is and how he is the essence of love and passion in a human being.

i. After the reading I summarize by referring back to the Aim.

j. I then assign the homework and ask for questions. Always ask if the students understand the homework assignment. This way they can't tell you the next day that they couldn't do the homework because they didn't understand it. (Now that you eliminated that excuse, you have to work on the others.)

Key Terms:

Petrarchan lover, sonnet, iambic pentameter, Globe Theater…

Summary:

Discuss how Romeo is unlike some young men today in the "romance department".

Why is he able to be labeled a Petrarchan lover?

Homework: Write a journal entry as Romeo at the beginning of the play.

Marc Hoberman

(School letterhead here)

To the parent of_____

Please note that your son/daughter is having trouble in the following areas.

_____ homework   _____ preparation
_____ classwork   _____ self control
_____ behavior   _____ testing
_____ language   _____ other

I am certain that if we work together, we can help _____ to improve his/her difficulties. Please feel free to contact me at _____ (insert SCHOOL phone number, SCHOOL email address, DEPARTMENT phone #, etc). If you would like to schedule a meeting, please let me know at your earliest convenience. Please sign this letter and have your child return it to me tomorrow.

Respectfully,

_____   _____
  Teacher Signature   Chairperson Signature
       Subject

_____
Parent Signature

Have your chairperson or AP sign the original and then you can make copies. You might want to make copies of all letters you send home to keep for your records. Having your chairperson sign is usually a good idea so he or she can troubleshoot any problems before they arise.

INSERT YOUR CLASS HEADING HERE

(Possible Contract for students and parents).

1. No foul language
2. No hats (Bad hair days are your problem, not mine.)
3. Raise your hand to ask or answer a question
4. Never throw your work out
5. Garbage gets thrown out at the end of the period (I hate when they get up and throw garbage away when I am teaching. It distracts me and is rude.)
6. You are responsible for all work even if you are absent
7. The period is over when I say so, the bell means nothing to me. (I do not allow kids to pack up before I dismiss class. Those who do are made to leave last.)
8. Bring a Loose-leaf Notebook, two pens and two pencils EVERY day.
(I don't lend pens, I rent supplies. They cost points or a phone call home. I used to take money but not anymore.)

I have them sign the contract and the parent signs as well. I then make copies of the contract and keep one set and return the others to the students. They have to keep it in their notebooks. I like to have an outline in front of me indicating the rules I would like to be in my contract. However, I allow the students to create some of the rules that will be part of the contract for several reasons:

4. Their rules are usually more stringent than mine.
5. They take class very seriously when they have taken part in the creation of the contract.
6. This allows them to have OWNERSHIP of some of the management of the classroom.

ADD YOUR GRADING POLICY HERE AS WELL AS TWO SPACES FOR STUDENT AND PARENT SIGNATURE.

_____   _____
        Student Signature   Parent Signature

Marc Hoberman

GRADEBOOK

QTR:_____CLASS:_____PD:____

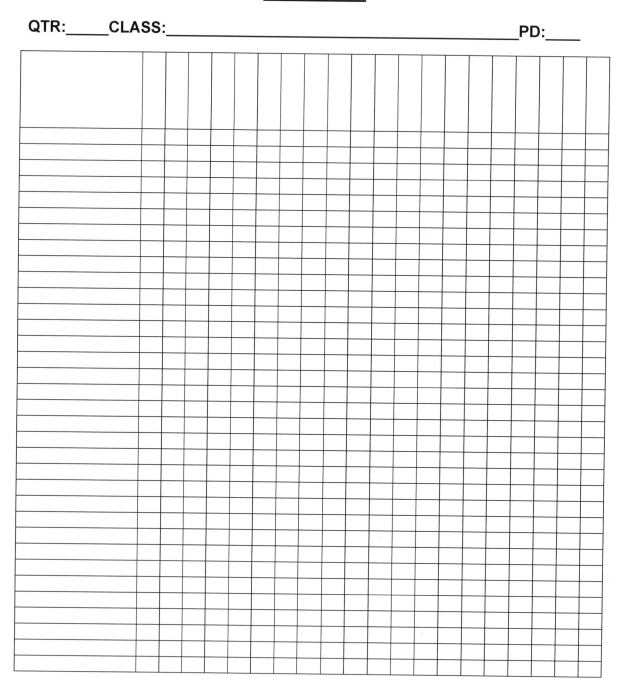

School Letterhead

Date:

Dear Parents or Guardians:

Your child is currently involved in studying_____

_____
(describe unit of study and class, if appropriate). It is our intention to use the
videotape_____(title)
on _____(date) because_____

_____
(describe the use of this videotape in relation to your academic goals and
objectives).

This letter is being sent to you in compliance with the District policy requiring
parents/guardians to approve the intended use of videotapes or films which are
not owned, broadcast, or recommended by the District prior to their scheduled
showing. As part of that policy, we ask you to complete the form below,
authorizing or exempting your child from the videotape showing. Please return
your completed form to your child's teacher. Students exempted from this
showing will be required to complete an alternative assignment. Should you
have any questions regarding the videotape, please contact me.

_____
Signature of principal

(From <u>Using Film in the High School Curriculum: A Practical Guide</u>
<u>For Teachers and Librarians</u> by Kenneth E. Resch and Vicki D. Schicker)

Marc Hoberman

Sample Form
_____ School District
_____School

Statement Regarding Videotape or Film Use

(For Material Which Is Not Owned, Broadcast, or Recommended by the District)

Date: _____

Teacher's Name_____ Room_____

Title or description of
program: _____
_____

Producer (if known): _____

Network (if known): _____

Material: Rented   _____

Purchased   _____

Taped at home   _____

Parental permission required: Yes_____ No_____

I plan to use the above program in my classroom on _____ (date)
for the following reason (describe its use in relation to your academic goals and objectives:
_____
_____

This program complies with the school's policy on the evaluation and selection of instructional materials. It is appropriate for the grade level and the instructional content enhances the curriculum. If this program has been recorded off-air, I affirm that it will be erased according to "fair use" interpretations of federal copyright regulations.

_____
Teacher's signature

Approved: _____   _____
            Principal's signature   Date

(From Using Film in the High School Curriculum: A Practical Guide For Teachers and Librarians by Kenneth E. Resch and Vicki D. Schicker)

Student Class Participation Worksheet Class_____Period____
(Students start with a grade of 100 and lose 5 points for each time a date is written in a particular box.)

Name	Pen or Pencil	Text Book	Notebook	Punctuality	Talking	Classwork

Marc Hoberman

<u>ATTENDANCE</u>

QTR:_____ CLASS:_____PD:____

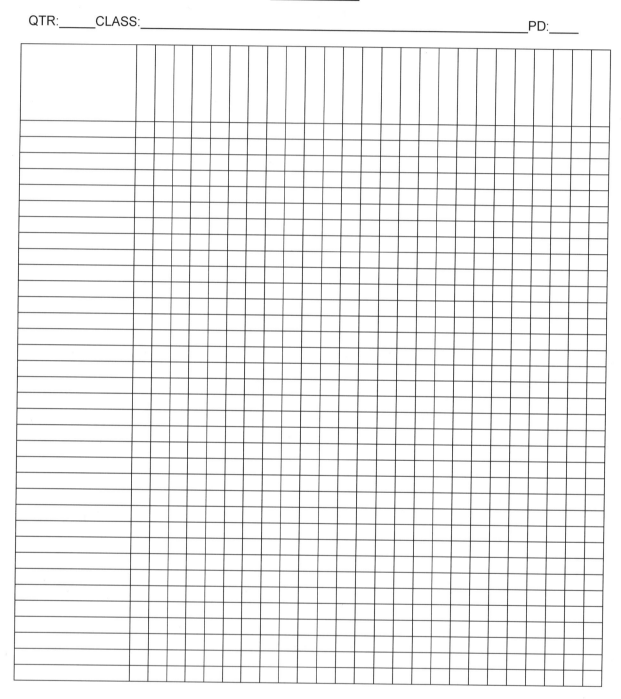

Websites for Lesson Plans

http://teachers.net/lessons/

http://www.edhelper.com/

http://www.teachnet.com/

http://www.teachnet.com/lesson/

http://www.education-world.com/a_tsl/

http://www.lessonplanspage.com/

http://www.lessonplanspage.com/

http://lessonplanz.com/

http://education.indiana.edu/cas/ttforum/lesson.html

http://www.atozteacherstuff.com/

http://www.pacificnet.net/~mandel/

http://www.askeric.org/Virtual/Lessons/

http://www.pbs.org/teachersource/

http://www.teachersfirst.com/

http://www.csun.edu/~hcedu013/plans.html

http://www.theteacherscorner.net/

http://www.col-ed.org/cur/

http://www.csun.edu/~vceed009/lesson.html

http://my.execpc.com/~dboals/k-12.html

http://www.constitutioncenter.org/sections/teacher/lesson_plans/lessons_main.asp

About the Author

Marc Hoberman is a teacher, motivational speaker, corporate trainer and coach. He has trained hundreds of teachers nationally and his techniques have been featured on television and radio. He is the owner of Grade Success, Inc. Tutoring Service and has developed a Speed Reading and Study Skills Course that has been used in several public and private schools. Marc was a featured speaker at the Young Adult Institute (YAI) International Conference, the New Jersey Reading Conference, and the New York State Reading Conference. Marc's Power Memorization Seminar has taught hundreds of students, teachers, parents and business professionals how to increase their memories and ability to retain information. His ability to help teachers improve in all aspects of their performance is unparalleled.